For Joshua, Ira & Jeff
& 1,001 GoodNights!

The Little Sheep Who Couldn't Sleep

Illustrations & Text ©1990-2011 Ilene Winn-Lederer

ISBN-10 0-615-45847-5
ISBN-13 9780615458472

1st Edition 2011
10 9 8 7 6 5 4 3 2 1

All Rights Reserved.
No part of this book may be used or reproduced in any manner
whatsoever or by any electronic or mechanical means, including
information storage and retrieval systems without prior written permission
of the publisher except in the case of brief quotations embodied in reviews.

Imaginarius Editions

986 Lilac Street
Pittsburgh, PA 15217
(412) 421-8668
ilene@winnlederer.com
www.winnlederer.com

The Little Sheep Who Couldn't Sleep

**Story & Pictures By
Ilene Winn-Lederer**

Imaginarius Editions
Pittsburgh

Once, when the moon was slim in the night sky, there was a little sheep who couldn't sleep.

For Willy, bedtime was the best time for reading and for thinking about all sorts of important things.

Like why his Ma-a and Da-ad put HIM to bed when only THEY were sleepy!

Sometimes Willy couldn't sleep because...

he was hungry and thirsty, or he needed just a little

bedtime story and a back-scratch.

When some Yawns came to visit, Willy just laughed...

... and the Yawns flew away!

If some Tosses and Turns wanted to play...

PIF! POF! PAF! Willy was ready for them.

Then, when everyone else was asleep, Willy listened...

For the crickets chirping their secret songs,

or for the hum of faraway traffic. He could even hear the trees whispering softly to the stars...

Suddenly, Willy heard something go "Pa-Thump, Pa-Thump" right past his window! WHAT could it be?

With his blanket for protection, the little sheep got out of his bed to investigate ...

"Aw–w–w," Willy sighed, rolling his eyes. "It's only old Mrs. Fleecekin out for her nightly run."

Willy watched her jog around the block. ONE time.

Then TWO times...

Now **THREE** times...
"Maybe she can't sleep either," thought Willy.

"Pa-Thump, Pa-Thump." Willy tapped the beat on his window sill. "I like that sound," he smiled.

FOUR times ...

FIVE times...

The little sheep waved as his neighbor flashed by.

SIX times...
Willy didn't see the Yawns sneaking back into his room.

SEVEN times...

He didn't see the Tosses and Turns slipping out from under his door...

EIGHT times...

A Yawn snuggled down with Willy on his pillow.

NINE times...

When Mrs. Fleecekin had jogged around the block TEN times, she stopped to wave back at Willy.

But where did that little sheep go?

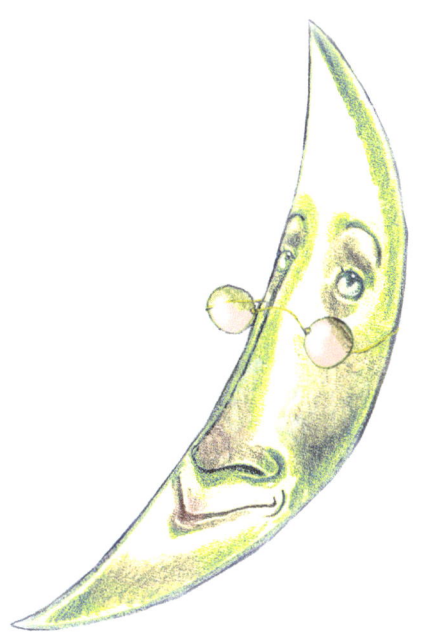

About The Author...

Ilene Winn-Lederer, author & illlustrator,
can usually be found hovering between a
mostly trusty iMac and a sometimes neat
drawing table in her tiny treetop studio, weaving
stories & ideas into whatever visual mischief
might light her fancy on the night you come to visit.

Other books from Imaginarius Editions:

The Alchymical Zoodiac: *A Celestial Bestiary* (2009)

Stitchburgh (2010)

Archival, signed prints of illustrations from **Imaginarius Editions**
are available from the publisher upon request. Contact: ilene@winnlederer.com

www.ingramcontent.com/pod-product-compliance
Lightning Source LLC
Chambersburg PA
CBHW042004150426
43194CB00002B/124